Oxford Progressive English Readers
General Editor: D.H. Howe

Five Tales

The *Oxford Progressive English Readers* series provides a wide range of reading for learners of English. It includes classics, the favourite stories of young readers, and also modern fiction. The series has five grades: the *Introductory Grade* at a 1400 word level, *Grade 1* at a 2100 word level, *Grade 2* at a 3100 word level, *Grade 3* at a 3700 word level and *Grade 4* which consists of abridged stories. Structural as well as lexical controls are applied at each level.

Wherever possible the mood and style of the original stories have been retained. Where this requires departure from the grading scheme, definitions and notes are given.

All the books in the series are attractively illustrated. Each book also has a short section containing questions and suggested activities for students.

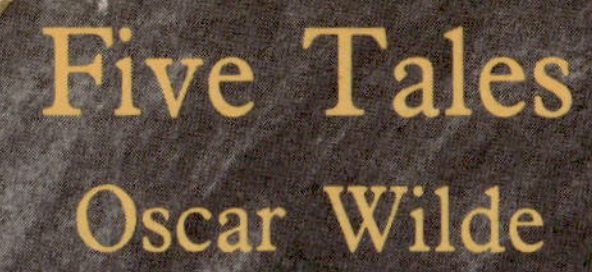

Five Tales

Oscar Wilde

Hong Kong
OXFORD UNIVERSITY PRESS
Oxford Singapore Tokyo

Oxford University Press

Oxford New York Toronto
Petaling Jaya Singapore Hong Kong Tokyo
Delhi Bombay Calcutta Madras Karachi
Nairobi Dar es Salaam Cape Town
Melbourne Auckland

and associated companies in
Berlin Ibadan

Retold by D. Fullerton and J. Oxley
Illustrated by R. Parsons
Cover illustration by Fung Ka
Simplified according to the language grading scheme
especially compiled by D.H. Howe

First published 1975
Sixteenth impression 1990

ISBN 0 19 580723 5

Printed in Hong Kong by Liang Yu Printing Factory Ltd.
Published by Oxford University Press, Warwick House, Hong Kong

Contents

1 The Happy Prince

The Happy Prince was a statue*. He stood very high above the city where everyone could see him. He was covered all over with leaves of gold. His eyes were two diamonds, and a large red ruby* shone on the top of his sword.

Everyone in the city enjoyed looking at him. 'He is very beautiful,' people said to each other. 'But he's not very useful, is he?'

'Why can't you be like the Happy Prince?' mothers said to their children if they cried. 'The Happy Prince never cries about anything.'

'I'm glad there is someone in the world who is quite happy,' said an angry old man, as he looked at the wonderful statue.

'He looks just like an angel*,' said the school-children as they came out of church.

'How do you know?' asked one of the school-masters. 'You have never seen one.'

'Ah, but we have in our dreams,' answered the children. The master looked angry, because he did not like children to dream too much.

The little bird

One night a little bird flew over the city. His friends had gone away to Egypt six weeks before, but he had stayed behind. He was in love with a beautiful water flower. He met her early in the spring, when he was flying down the river chasing a big yellow insect. He stopped to talk to her, but of course she could not answer him. After a while he grew tired of her, and decided to follow his friends to Egypt.

**statue*, likeness of a person made of wood or stone.
**ruby*, a precious jewel.
**angel*, messenger from God (usually shown in pictures as a man with white wings).

He flew all day, and at night he arrived at the city. 'Where shall I stay?' he asked as he looked around him.

Then he saw the statue, standing high above the city.

'I will sleep there,' he cried. 'It is a fine place with plenty of fresh air.' So he flew down and landed between the feet of the Happy Prince.

'I have a golden bedroom,' he said to himself as he looked around. He got ready to go to sleep. Just as he was closing his eyes, a large drop of water fell on him.

'That's very strange,' he cried. 'There is not a cloud in the sky, and yet it is raining.' Then another drop fell. 'What is the use of a statue if it cannot keep the rain off?' he said. 'I must look for another place to sleep.'

Just at that moment another drop fell. He looked up and saw something very strange.

The Happy Prince cries

The eyes of the Happy Prince were filled with tears. Tears were running down his golden face. He looked so beautiful in the moonlight that the little bird was really sorry for him.

'Who are you?' he asked.

'I am the Happy Prince.'

'Why are you crying, then?' asked the bird. 'You have made me very wet with your tears.'

'When I was alive, and had a human heart,' answered the statue, 'I did not know what sorrow was. I lived in a beautiful palace* where there was never any sadness. In the daytime I played with my friends in the garden. At night I danced in the palace. All around the garden was a high wall. I never knew what was on the other side of it. Everything around me was very beautiful. My friends called me the Happy Prince, and I was. Then I died, and people put me up here so that I could see all the ugliness and unhappiness of my city. And although my heart is made of lead*, I cannot help crying.'

'What! Isn't he made of gold all the way through?' thought

**palace*, house of a king.
**lead*, heavy, soft, grey metal.

the bird to himself. He was too polite to say such a thing aloud.

The poor mother

The statue began to speak again.

'Far away in a little street there is a poor house,' he said. 'One of the windows is open, and I can see a woman sitting at a table. Her face is thin and she looks worried. In a bed in a corner of the room, her little boy is lying ill. He is asking for oranges. His mother has nothing to give him but river water, so he is crying. Little bird, will you take her the ruby from the top of my sword?'

'My friends are waiting for me in Egypt,' said the bird, 'I must go to them.'

'Little bird,' said the Prince, 'please stay with me for just one night and be my messenger. The boy is so thirsty and the mother so sad.'

'I don't think I like little boys,' answered the bird. 'Last summer, when I was staying by the river, there were two boys who threw stones at me. They never hit me, I flew too fast, but it was not very pleasant.'

But the Prince looked so sad that the little bird was sorry.

'It is very cold here,' he said, 'but I will stay with you for one night and be your messenger.'

'Thank you, little bird,' said the Prince.

So the bird picked the big ruby out of the Prince's sword. He flew away with it in his beak, over the roofs of the town.

He flew by the palace and heard the sound of dancing. He flew over the river and saw all the ships ready to sail away. He flew over crowded shops, and saw people buying and selling. At last he came to the poor house and looked in. The boy was lying ill on his bed, and the mother had fallen asleep. In he flew, and put the big ruby on the table beside the woman's hand. Then he flew around the bed, cooling the boy's head with his wings.

'How cool I feel!' said the boy. 'I must be getting better,' and he went to sleep.

Then the bird flew back to the Happy Prince and told him what he had done.

'I don't know why,' he said, 'but I feel quite warm now, although it is so cold.'

'That is because you have helped someone,' said the Prince. The little bird soon fell asleep.

The bird wants to leave

Early next morning, the bird flew down to the river and had a bath.

'How strange,' said a professor as he was passing over the

bridge. 'That kind of bird, here, in winter!' And he wrote a long letter to the newspaper. Everyone talked about it. It was so unusual.

'Tonight I shall go to Egypt,' said the bird. He visited all the buildings in the city, and sat on the top of the church tower for a long time. Everywhere he went, the other birds looked at him and said, 'What a fine stranger!' When the moon rose he flew back to the Happy Prince.

'Have you any messages for Egypt?' he cried. 'I am just starting.'

'Little bird,' said the Prince, 'please stay with me for one night longer.'

'My friends are waiting for me in Egypt,' said the bird. 'The sun is shining and the air is warm. I must go.'

'Little bird,' said the Prince, 'far away across the city I see a young man in a small room. He is leaning over a table covered with papers. In a glass by his side is a bunch of dead flowers. He is trying to finish a play for the theatre, but he is too cold to write any more. There is no fire in the room, and he is weak from hunger.'

'I will wait with you for one more night,' said the bird, who was very kind. 'Shall I take him another ruby?'

'I have no ruby now,' said the Prince, 'my eyes are all I have left. They are made of precious diamonds. Pull one of them out and take it to him. He will sell it, and buy firewood and food and then finish his play.'

'Dear Prince,' said the bird, 'I cannot do that,' and he began to cry.

'Little bird,' said the Prince, 'do as I command you.'

The bird takes the diamond

So the bird took out the Prince's eye, and flew away to the young man's room.

It was easy to get in, for there was a hole in the roof. The young man had his head buried in his hands, so that he did not see the bird. When he looked up he found the beautiful diamond lying on the dead flowers.

'This must be from someone who likes my plays,' he cried. 'Now I can finish the one I am writing,' and he looked very happy.

Next day the bird flew down to the harbour. He watched a large ship sail away and heard the sailors shouting to one another.

'I am going to Egypt,' cried the bird, but nobody cared. When the moon rose he flew back to the Happy Prince.

'I have come to say good-bye to you,' he cried.

'Little bird,' said the Prince, 'please stay with me for one more night.'

'It is winter,' answered the bird, 'and snow will soon be here. In Egypt the sun is warm on the green trees. My friends are building a nest, and the pink and white birds are watching them. Dear Prince, I must leave you, but I will never forget you. Next spring I will bring you back two beautiful jewels in place of those you have given away. The ruby will be redder than a red rose, and the diamond will be as white as snow.'

The little match-girl

'In the street below us,' said the Happy Prince, 'is a little match-girl. She has dropped all her matches in the dirty street and they are spoiled. Her father will beat her if she does not bring home some money, and she is crying. Take out my other eye and give it to her. Then her father will not beat her.'

'I will stay with you one night longer,' said the bird, 'but I cannot take out your eye. You would be completely blind then.'

'Little bird,' said the Prince, 'do as I command you.'

So he took out the Prince's other eye, and went off with it in his beak. He flew past the match-girl and slipped the diamond into her hand.

'What a lovely piece of glass,' cried the girl, and she ran home laughing.

Then the bird came back to the Prince.

'You are blind now,' he said, 'so I will stay with you for ever.'

'No, little bird,' said the Prince, 'you must go away to Egypt.'

'I will stay with you always,' said the bird, and he slept at the Prince's feet.

The bird stays with the Prince

5 The next day he sat on the Prince's shoulder and told him stories of what he had seen in strange lands. He told him of the great red birds that stand in rows on the banks of the Nile, waiting to catch golden fish in their beaks. He told him about the merchants who walk slowly across the desert with their 10 camels*. He spoke about the great green snake that sleeps in a palm-tree, and has twenty men to feed it with sweet cakes.

'Dear little bird,' said the Prince, 'you tell me of wonderful things, but I am more interested in the sadness of my own people. Fly over my city, little bird, and tell me what you 15 see.'

So the bird flew over the great city. He saw the rich people living happily in their beautiful houses, while beggars were sitting at their gates. He saw the white faces of hungry children looking out from their dark houses. Under a bridge, two 20 little boys were sitting close together to try and keep warm.

'How hungry we are,' they said.

'You can't stay here,' shouted the watchman, and he sent them out into the rain.

The bird flew back and told the Prince what he had seen.

25 'I am covered with gold,' said the Prince. 'You must take it off, leaf by leaf, and give it to the poor people.'

The bird helps the poor

The bird took off the gold, leaf by leaf, till the Prince looked quite dull and grey. He took the gold to the poor, and the children's faces grew healthier. They laughed once more, 30 and played games in the streets.

'We have bread now!' they cried.

The snow came and the air was very cold. The streets shone like silver. Ice hung down from the houses and everybody wore warm fur coats.

**camel*, a large animal used for carrying heavy loads in the desert.

The poor little bird grew colder and colder, but he would not leave the Prince. At last, he knew he was going to die. He had just enough strength left to fly up to the Prince's shoulder once more.

'Good-bye, dear Prince,' he said. 'Will you let me kiss your hand?'

'I am glad you are going to Egypt at last,' said the Prince. 'You have stayed here too long. But you must give me a good-bye kiss, for I love you.'

'I am not going to Egypt,' said the bird. 'I am going to the House of Death.' He kissed the Prince and fell down dead at his feet.

At that moment a strange crack sounded inside the statue as if something had broken. It was the lead heart of the statue. It had broken in two. It certainly was a cold night.

The statue is pulled down

Early next morning the Mayor was walking in the street below, with the Town Councillors. As they passed the statue, he looked up at it.

'Oh dear, how old and dirty the Happy Prince looks,' he said.

'Oh, yes!' said the Town Councillors, who always agreed with the Mayor. They went up to look at it.

'The ruby has fallen out of his sword, his eyes are gone, and he is no longer golden,' said the Mayor. 'He is no better than a beggar.'

'No better than a beggar,' repeated the Town Councillors.

'And there is a dead bird at his feet, too. We really must not allow that to happen in future.'

So they pulled down the statue of the Happy Prince.

'He is no longer beautiful, so he is no longer useful,' they said.

Then they melted the statue in a fire, and the Mayor held a meeting to decide what was to be done with the metal.

'We must have another statue, of course,' he said, 'and it shall be a statue of myself.'

'Of myself,' said each of the Town Councillors, and they

quarrelled. When I last heard of them, they were still quarrelling.

'What a strange thing!' they said, when the statue of the Happy Prince was being melted. 'This broken lead heart will 5 not melt in the fire. We must throw it away.' So they threw it on a dust-heap where the dead bird was also lying.

'Bring me the two most precious things in the city,' said God to one of his Angels. The Angel brought him the lead heart and the dead bird.

10 'You have chosen rightly,' said God. 'This little bird shall sing for ever in my garden in Heaven, and in my city of gold, the Happy Prince shall honour me.'

2 The Star-child

Long ago, two poor woodcutters were going home through a great forest. It was winter and the night was very cold. There was thick snow on the ground and on the branches of the trees. The river was quite frozen.

On and on the two woodcutters went, blowing hard on their fingers to keep their hands warm. They fell into the deep snow and came out looking quite white. Their wood fell out of their arms and they had to stop to tie it up again. Once, they thought that they had lost their way, and they were very frightened. But at last they reached the edge of the forest. They could see, far away, the lights of the village where they lived. They were so happy to be out of the forest that they began to laugh aloud.

The Star-child

The two men stood talking for a while, when suddenly a strange thing happened. A very bright and beautiful star fell from the sky. As they watched it, it seemed to fall behind some trees that stood close by.

'Ah! There is a pot of gold for the man that finds it,' they cried, and they ran, because they were so pleased at the thought of finding the gold.

One of them ran faster than his friend, and came to the other side of the trees. There was something gold lying on the white snow. So he ran towards it, and found a golden coat, covered with silver stars. He called out to his friend that he had found the gold that had fallen from the sky. When his friend joined him, they sat down in the snow ready to divide the gold which they were sure the coat contained. But when they opened it up there was no gold in it, nor silver, nor money of any kind. There was only a little child who was asleep.

They were very disappointed. 'This is not what we hoped for,' said one. 'What can we do with another child, when we have no money? We have children of our own to feed. Let us leave it here.'

But his friend answered, 'No, it would be an evil thing to leave it here to die in the snow. I have as many children as you to feed, and I am just as poor. But I will take it home with me and my wife shall look after it.'

At the woodcutter's house

So he carefully picked up the child and wrapped the coat around it to keep it warm. Then he walked on to the village with his friend, who wondered how he could be so foolish.

When they came to the village, his friend said to him, 'You have the child, so give me the golden coat, for we should share what we find.'

But he answered, 'No. The coat is not mine or yours. It belongs to the child,' and he said good-bye, went to his own house and knocked on the door.

The door was opened by his wife, who was very happy that her husband had returned safely. She put her arms round his neck and kissed him, then took the wood from him and told him to come in.

But he said to her, 'I have found something in the forest, and I have brought it home so that you can look after it.' He did not move away from the door.

'What is it?' she cried. 'Show it to me, for the house is empty and we need many things.' And he opened the coat and showed her the sleeping child.

'Oh, my husband!' she said. 'We have enough children of our own without you bringing another from the forest. It may bring us bad luck. And how shall we look after it?' And she was very angry with him.

'But it is a Star-child,' he answered, and told her how he had found it.

His wife was still angry. 'Our own children have no bread, why should we have to feed a child belonging to somebody else?' she cried.

The man did not answer, but remained standing outside the open door. A terribly cold wind came in from the forest through the open door. His wife said to him, 'Will you please shut the door. The wind is blowing into the house and I am cold.'

'A cold wind always comes into a house where someone is unkind,' he said. And the woman said nothing, but moved closer to the fire.

After a time she turned round and looked at him. There were tears in her eyes. He came in quickly and placed the child in her arms. She kissed it, and laid it in the bed where the youngest of their own children was lying. The next day, the woodcutter took the golden coat and the amber* necklace* that the child was wearing, and put them away.

The Star-child grows up

So the Star-child grew up with the woodcutter's children. He ate with them and played with them. And every year he became more beautiful to look at. The people who lived in the village were curious about him. They were all dark and black-haired, but he was white and his hair was fair. He looked like a golden flower.

Yet his beauty did him no good, for he became proud and cruel. He laughed at the woodcutter's children, and the other children of the village, because they were poor. He told them that he was noble, the child of a star. So he made himself their master, and called them his servants. He had no pity for the blind, or those who were poor and ill. Instead, he threw stones at them and ordered them to leave the village. He loved only beauty, and would make fun of all weak and ugly creatures. He loved himself, and in the summer he would lie by the well in the garden, and laugh with pleasure at the sight of his own lovely face.

The woodcutter and his wife often said to him, 'Why are you so cruel to others? That is not the way we treated you when we found you, a baby in the snow.'

But the Star-child took no notice of their words and went

**amber*, hard yellow-coloured gum, used for making ornaments.
**necklace*, jewels worn around the neck.

angrily back to his friends. And they followed him everywhere, for he could run and dance and make music. And wherever the Star-child led them, they followed. Whatever the Star-child told them to do, they did.

5 *The beggar-woman*

One day, a poor beggar-woman passed through the village. Her clothes were old and torn, and her feet were scratched and bleeding because she had no shoes. She was very tired, so she sat down under a tree to rest.

10 When the Star-child saw her, he said to his friends, 'Look, there is an awful beggar-woman under that lovely green tree. She is ugly and dirty. Come with me and let us send her away.'

So he came near, and threw stones at her, and laughed at 15 her. She looked at him with fear in her eyes. And when the woodcutter, who was working nearby, saw what the Star-child was doing, he ran up to stop him. 'What has this poor woman done to you so that you treat her like this? Leave her alone!' he said.

20 And the Star-child grew red with anger and said, 'Who are you to question what I do? I am not your son. You cannot tell me what to do.'

'You are right,' answered the woodcutter, 'yet I was kind to you when I found you in the forest.'

25 When the beggar-woman heard these words, she gave a loud cry, and fell down. The woodcutter carried her into his own house, and his wife took care of her. When she felt better, they brought her some food.

But she would not eat or drink. 'Did you say you found 30 the child in the forest?' she asked. 'Was it ten years ago today?'

And the woodcutter answered, 'Yes, it was in the forest that I found him, and it was ten years ago today.'

'And what did you find with him?' she cried. 'Was he 35 wearing an amber necklace? Did he have a golden coat with stars on it?'

'Yes,' answered the woodcutter, 'he had those things when I found him.' And he took the golden coat and the necklace and showed them to her.

The Star-child's mother

When she saw them she cried for joy, and said, 'He is my little son, whom I lost in the forest. Please, send him to me at once, for I have wandered all over the world looking for him.' 5

So the woodcutter and his wife went and called to the Star-child, and said to him, 'Go into the house. There you will find your mother, who is waiting for you.' 10

He ran in feeling glad and full of joy. But when he saw the woman waiting there, he laughed and said, 'Why, where is my mother? I see no one here but this old beggar-woman.'

And the woman answered, 'I am your mother.'

'You must be mad,' cried the Star-child angrily. 'I am not your son, for you are an ugly beggar. Go away from here, and never let me see your face again.' 15

'Oh, but you are my little son, whom I lost in the forest,' she cried. She fell on her knees and held out her arms to him. 'The robbers stole you from me, and left you to die,' she said. 'But I knew you when I saw you and when I heard about the golden coat and the amber necklace. Come with me now, for I have wandered all over the world looking for you. Come with me, my son, for I need your love.' 20

But the Star-child did not move from his place. The only sound that was heard was the sound of the woman crying. 25

At last he spoke to her, and his voice was hard. 'If you are really my mother,' he said, 'it would have been better if you had stayed away. I thought I was the child of some star, and not a beggar's child, as you tell me I am. Go away, and never let me see you again.' 30

'Oh, my son!' she cried. 'Will you kiss me before I go? For I have suffered so much to find you.'

'No,' said the Star-child, 'for you are too ugly. I would rather kiss a snake or a toad* than you.' 35

**toad*, an animal like a frog.

The Star-child is changed

So the woman went away into the forest. When the Star-child saw that she had gone, he was glad, and ran back to his friends.

But when they saw him coming, they said, 'Why, you are as dirty as a toad and as ugly as a snake. Go away, we will not let you play with us.'

And the Star-child was very surprised, and said to himself, 'What are they saying to me? What do they mean? I will go to the well and look at myself in the water.'

He went straight to the well and looked into it. In the water he saw his own reflection. His face was like the face of a toad, and his body was like that of a snake. He sat down on the grass and cried, and said to himself, 'This must have happened because of my wickedness. I have sent my mother away, and been proud and cruel to her. I will go and search for her through the whole world, and I will not rest until I find her.'

The little daughter of the woodcutter came to him and, 'It doesn't matter if you are ugly now. Stay with us and I will not laugh at you, nor be unkind.'

'No. I have been cruel to my mother, and now I am being punished. I must go and find her, so that I can ask her to forgive me,' said the Star-child.

The Star-child searches for his mother

He ran into the forest, and called out to his mother to come to him, but there was no answer. All day long he called to her, and at night he lay down to sleep on a bed of leaves. The birds and animals ran away from him, for they remembered how cruel he was.

In the morning he went on through the great forest. He asked everything he met whether they had seen his mother. But none of the birds or animals would tell him, for he had been so cruel to them.

The Star-child cried, and asked God's creatures to forgive him, and went on through the forest looking for the beggar-woman. On the third day he came to the other side of the forest, and could see the plains* stretching before him.

When he went down into the villages, the children laughed at him and threw stones at him. No one could tell him anything about the beggar-woman who was his mother. For three years he wandered over the world, and often seemed to see her on the road in front of him. He called out to her, and ran after her until his feet were cut and sore. But he could never find her.

At the gate of the city

One evening, he came to the gate of a walled city that stood by a river. Although he was tired, he tried to enter. But the soldiers who were guarding the gate said roughly to him, 'What do you want in the city?'

'I am looking for my mother,' he answered, 'please let me in, for perhaps she is here, inside the gates.'

But they laughed at him, and one of them cried, 'Your mother will not be pleased when she sees you. You are uglier than a toad and dirtier than a snake. Go away from here, your mother does not live in this city.' And another said, 'Who is your mother and why are you searching for her?'

'My mother is a beggar, like me,' he answered. 'I have treated her badly. Let me in so that she may forgive me, if she is in the city.' But they would not let him pass.

As he turned away crying, a rich man came to the gates, and he asked the soldiers who it was that wished to come into the city. 'It is a beggar, the child of a beggar,' they told him, 'and we have sent him away.'

'No,' cried the rich man, laughing. 'We shall sell the ugly thing. He will be a slave, and he will be sold for the price of a bowl of sweet wine.'

The Star-child is sold

And an old, evil-faced man who was passing by called out and said, 'I shall buy him for that price.' He paid the money, and took the Star-child by the hand, and led him into the

**plains,* area of flat country.

city. After they had gone through many streets, they came to a little door in a wall. The old man touched the door with the ring on his finger and it opened. They went down five brass* steps into a garden full of black flowers and great green pots. The old man took a piece of silk, and tied it over the Star-child's eyes, and pushed him along. When the silk was taken off, he found himself in a dark prison.

The old man gave him some dry bread and said, 'Eat,' and some salt water and said, 'Drink.' When the Star-child had eaten and drunk, the old man went out, locking the door behind him, and fastening it with an iron chain.

The three pieces of gold

Now, the old man who had bought the Star-child, was one of the most evil magicians* in the city. Next morning, he came to the prison where he had locked up the Star-child, and said to him, 'In a wood near the gate of this city, are three pieces of gold. One is white gold, and another is yellow gold. The third piece is red. Today you will bring me the piece of white gold. If you do not bring it back, I will beat you. Go quickly, and at sunset I shall be waiting for you at the door of the garden. Make sure you bring me the piece of white gold, or you will be sorry. For I bought you for the price of a bowl of sweet wine, and you are my slave.'

He tied the piece of silk over the Star-child's eyes, and led him through the house. They went through the garden of black flowers and up the five brass steps. The magician opened the door with his ring and pushed the Star-child out into the street.

The Star-child went out of the gate of the city and soon came to the wood that his master had told him about.

The wood was very lovely to look at from the outside. It seemed full of singing birds and flowers. The Star-child entered it gladly. Yet when he was inside, he found great plants covered with thorns* which hurt him when he moved.

**brass,* yellow metal.
**magician,* a person skilled in magic tricks.
**thorns,* sharp points which grow on some plants.

He could not find the piece of white gold anywhere, though he searched from morning till noon, and from noon to sunset. At last he turned towards the city, crying, for he knew what would happen to him.

The little rabbit

But when he reached the edge of the wood, he heard a cry. It sounded like something in pain. Forgetting his own troubles, he turned back and ran towards the sound. He found a little rabbit caught in a trap that some hunter had set for it. *5*

The Star-child was very sorry for it, and set it free. 'Thank you,' said the rabbit. 'You have given me my freedom, now what can I give you in return?' *10*

The Star-child said, 'I am searching for a piece of white gold, but I cannot find it anywhere. If I do not take it to my master he will beat me.'

'Come with me,' said the rabbit. 'I know where it is hidden.' So the Star-child went with the rabbit, and found the piece of white gold hidden in a hole in a tree. He was very happy, and said to the rabbit, 'You have repaid my kindness a hundred times over.' *15*

'No,' answered the rabbit. 'I treated you as you treated me,' and it ran away quickly. The Star-child went towards the city. *20*

The sick beggar

Just outside the gate of the city sat a sick beggar. When he saw the Star-child coming, he called out to him, 'Give me a piece of money, or I shall die of hunger. They have thrown me out of the city, and there is no one to help me.' *25*

'But I have only one piece of money with me,' said the Star-child, 'and if I do not bring it to my master he will beat me.'

The beggar cried and cried, until at last the Star-child gave him the piece of white gold. *30*

When he came to the Magician's door, the Magician was waiting for him, and took him inside. 'Have you brought the piece of white gold?' he asked. And the Star-child answered, 'I have not.' So the Magician beat him and put before him an empty plate, and said, 'Eat.' Then he gave him an empty cup and said, 'Drink,' and threw him into the dark prison.

Next morning the Magician came to him, and said, 'If you do not bring me the piece of yellow gold, I will keep you as my slave, and beat you again.'

So the Star-child went to the wood, and all day long he searched for the piece of yellow gold. But he could not find it anywhere. At sunset he sat down and began to cry.

The rabbit helps again

As he sat there crying, the little rabbit came to him again. 'Why are you crying?' asked the rabbit. 'And what are you looking for in the wood?'

'I am searching for a piece of yellow gold,' answered the Star-child. 'It is hidden here, and if I do not find it, my master will beat me, and keep me as his slave.'

'Follow me,' cried the little rabbit, and it ran through the wood until it came to a pool of water. At the bottom of the pool was the yellow piece of gold.

'How shall I thank you?' said the Star-child, 'for this is the second time you have helped me.' And he took the piece of yellow gold and hurried to the city.

But the beggar saw him coming, and ran to meet him. He fell on his knees and cried, 'Give me a piece of money, or I shall die of hunger.'

And the Star-child said to him, 'I have only a piece of yellow gold, and if I do not bring it to my master he will beat me, and keep me as his slave.'

But the sick beggar asked him again and again, so that at last the Star-child gave him the piece of yellow gold.

When he came to the Magician's door, the Magician was waiting for him. He took him inside and said to him, 'Have you the piece of yellow gold?' And the Star-child said, 'I have not.' So the Magician beat him again, and put chains on him and threw him into the dark prison.

And the next day the Magician came to him and said, 'If you bring me the piece of red gold today, I will set you free. But if you do not bring it, I will kill you.'

So the Star-child went to the wood, and all day long he searched for the piece of red gold, but he could not find it anywhere. And at sunset he sat down and cried, and as he was crying the little rabbit came to him. *5*

And the rabbit said to him, 'The piece of red gold that you are searching for is in the cave* behind you. So do not cry any more, but be glad.' *10*

'How shall I return your kindness?' cried the Star-child, 'for this is the third time that you have helped me.'

'Ah, but you helped me first,' said the rabbit, and ran quickly away.

The Star-child went into the cave, and in a corner he found the piece of red gold. He took it and hurried to the city. Again the beggar saw him coming, and stood in the middle of the road. He cried out, 'Give me the piece of red money, or I must die.' And the Star-child gave him the piece of red gold, saying, 'Your need is greater than mine.' Yet he was very unhappy, because he remembered what the Magician had said. *15* *20*

The Star-child is a Prince

But as he passed through the gates of the city, the guards bowed down and said, 'How beautiful is this young man. He must be a lord.'

A crowd of people followed him and said, 'Surely there is no one so beautiful in the whole world.' *25*

But the Star-child said to himself, 'They are laughing at me, and making fun of my unhappiness.' The crowd was so large that he lost his way, and found himself at last in a great open space in front of the palace of a king. *30*

The gates of the palace opened, and the priests and high officers of the city ran out to meet him. They bowed low and said, 'You are our lord for whom we have been waiting, and the son of our king.'

**cave*, a large hole in a rock wall.

The Star-child said, 'I am not a king's son, but the child of a poor beggar-woman. Why do you say that I am beautiful, for I know that I am evil to look at?'

Then one of the guards held up his shield and cried, 'See! 5 Now does my lord say that he is not beautiful?'

And the Star-child looked, and his face was as it had been when he was a child. His eyes were kinder, and his beauty had returned.

And the priests and the high officers knelt down and said, 10 'It was told long ago that on this day a man should come here who was to rule over us. Therefore, take this crown* and be our king.'

But he said to them, 'I cannot, for I have treated my mother wickedly, and I cannot rest until I find her and ask 15 her to forgive me. So let me go, for I must wander again over the world, and may not remain here, even if you give me the crown.'

The Star-child finds his mother

And as he spoke, he turned away from them towards the street that led to the gate of the city. Then, suddenly, 20 amongst the crowd that pressed round the soldiers, he saw the woman who was his mother. At her side was the sick beggar, who had sat by the road.

With a cry of joy, he ran over, and kissed his mother's feet and wetted them with his tears. He bowed his head to the 25 ground, and crying as if his heart might break, he said to her, 'Mother, I treated you wickedly. Forgive me.' But the woman did not answer him.

And he reached out his hands and said to the beggar, 'I helped you three times. Ask my mother to speak to me once.' 30 But the beggar said nothing.

And he cried again and said, 'Mother, my suffering is greater than I can bear. Forgive me and let me go back to the forest.' And the beggar-woman put her hand on his head and said, 'Rise,' and the beggar-man put his hand on his head and 35 said, 'Rise,' also.

**crown*, a jewelled head-dress worn by a king.

He stood up and looked at them and saw that they were a king and queen.

The Queen said to him, 'This is your father, whom you helped.'

5 The King said, 'This is your mother, whose feet you have washed with your tears.'

Then they kissed him, and brought him into the palace and put beautiful clothes on him. They put the crown on his head, and the sceptre in his hand and he was the King of the 10 city. He was a good king. He sent the evil Magician far away, and sent the woodcutter and his family many rich presents. He would not allow anyone to be cruel to animals or birds, but taught love and kindness to all. He gave food and clothing to the poor, and there was peace and plenty in the land.

15 Yet he did not rule for long. His suffering had been so great that after three years he died. And the King who ruled after him, ruled wickedly.

3 The Selfish* Giant

Every afternoon, when the children came out of school, they used to go and play in the Giant's garden.

It was a lovely garden, with soft green grass. Here and there over the grass were flowers like stars. There were about twelve peach trees that were covered in pink flowers in spring, and in autumn they had beautiful fruit. The birds sang sweetly on the trees, and all the children used to stop their games so that they could listen to them. 'How happy we are!' they cried to each other.

One day the Giant came back. He had been to visit another giant in Cornwall, and had stayed with him for seven years. When he arrived he saw all the children playing in the garden.

'What are you doing?' he cried in a very deep voice, and the children ran away.

'This garden belongs to me,' said the Giant. 'Nobody is allowed to play in it except myself.' So he built a high wall all round it, and put up a notice-board saying 'Keep out.'

He was a very selfish Giant.

Now the poor children had nowhere to play. They tried to play on the road, but the road was very dusty and full of hard stones, and they did not like it. They used to wander round the high walls when school was over, and talk about the beautiful garden inside. 'How happy we were there!' they said to each other.

Then the Spring came, and all over the country there were little flowers and little birds. But in the Selfish Giant's garden it was still winter. The birds did not want to sing in it as there were no children, and the trees forgot to flower. Once, a beautiful flower put its head out from the grass. But when it saw the notice-board, it was so sorry for the children that it slipped back into the ground again, and went off to sleep.

**selfish*, thinking of one's own needs, without care for others.

The only people who were pleased were the Snow and the Frost*.

'Spring has forgotten this garden,' they cried, 'so we will live here all the year round.'

5 The Snow covered up the grass with her great white coat, and the Frost painted all the trees silver. Then they invited the North Wind to stay with them, and he came. He was wrapped in furs, and all day he roared around the garden. He blew the chimney pots down from the roof.

10 'This is a lovely place,' he said, 'we must ask the Hail* to visit us.' So the Hail came. Every day for three hours he danced on the roof of the castle, and then he ran round and round the garden as fast as he could go. He was dressed in grey, and his breath was like ice.

15 'I cannot understand why the Spring is so late in coming,' said the Selfish Giant, as he sat by his window and looked out at his cold, white garden. 'I hope there will soon be a change in the weather.'

But the Spring never came, nor the Summer. The Autumn 20 gave golden fruit to every garden, but to the Giant's garden she gave none. 'He is too selfish,' she said. So it was always Winter there, and the North Wind, Hail, Frost and Snow danced about through the trees.

One morning the Giant was lying awake in bed when he 25 heard some lovely music. It sounded so beautiful that he thought it must be the King's musicians passing by. It was really only a little bird singing outside his window, but it was so long since he had heard a bird sing in his garden that it seemed to him to be the most beautiful music in the world. 30 Then the Hail stopped dancing over his head, and the North Wind stopped roaring. A wonderful smell came to him through the open window.

'I believe the Spring has come at last,' said the Giant, and he jumped out of bed and looked out.

35 What did he see?

******frost,* **thin ice on ground, roofs, plants, etc. caused by very cold weather.**

******hail,* **frozen raindrops falling from the sky.**

The children return

He saw the most wonderful sight. Through a hole in the wall, the children had crept in, and they were sitting in the branches of the trees. In every tree that he could see there was a little child. And the trees were so glad to have the children back again that they had covered themselves with flowers, and were moving their arms gently above the children's heads. The birds were flying about and singing with joy, and the flowers were looking up through the green grass and laughing.

It was a lovely scene, but in one corner it was still winter. It was the farthest corner of the garden, and in it stood a little boy. He was so small that he could not reach up to the branches of the tree, and he was wandering all round it, crying. The poor tree was still covered with frost and snow, and the North Wind was blowing and roaring above it. 'Climb up, little boy,' said the tree, and it bent its branches down as low as it could, but the boy was too tiny.

'How selfish I have been,' said the Giant as he looked out. 'Now I know why the Spring would not come here. I will put that poor little boy on the top of the tree, and then I will knock down the wall. My garden shall be the children's playground for ever and ever.' He was really very sorry for what he had done.

So he crept downstairs and opened the door quite softly, and went out into the garden. But when the children saw him they were so frightened that they all ran away, and the garden became winter again. Only the little boy did not run for his eyes were so full of tears that he did not see the Giant coming. And the Giant crept up behind him and took him gently in his hand, and put him into the tree. At once the tree put out its blossom, and the birds came and sang on it. The little boy stretched out his arms, put them round the Giant's neck and kissed him. When the other children saw that the Giant was not wicked any longer, they came running back, and with them came the Spring.

'It is your garden now, little children,' said the Giant, and he took a great axe and knocked down the wall. And when the people were going to market at twelve o'clock, they found the Giant playing with the children in the most beautiful garden they had ever seen.

All day long they played, and in the evening they came to say good-bye to the Giant.

'But where is your little friend?' he asked. 'The

boy I put up in the tree?' The Giant loved him the best because he had kissed him.

'We do not know,' answered the children, 'he has gone away.'

5 'You must tell him to come tomorrow,' said the Giant. But the children said that they did not know where he lived and had never seen him before, and the Giant felt very sad.

Every afternoon, when school was over, the children came and played with the Giant. But the little boy whom the Giant 10 loved was never seen again. The Giant was very kind to all the children, yet he longed to see his first little friend, and often spoke of him. 'How I would like to see him!' he used to say.

Years went by and the Giant grew very old and weak. He could not play about any more, so he sat in a huge arm-chair, 15 and watched the children, and admired his garden.

'I have many beautiful flowers,' he said, 'but the children are the most beautiful flowers of all.'

One winter morning he looked out of his window as he was dressing. He did not hate the Winter now, for he knew it 20 would soon be Spring again, and that the flowers were resting.

Suddenly he rubbed his eyes in wonder and looked and looked. It certainly was a wonderful sight. In the farthest corner of the garden was a tree quite covered with lovely white flowers. Its branches were golden, and silver fruit hung 25 down from them. There, underneath it, stood the little boy he had loved.

The Giant ran downstairs joyfully. He ran out into the garden and hurried across the grass towards the child. When he came quite close his face grew red with anger, and he said, 30 'Who has dared to hurt you?' For on the palms of the child's hands were the prints of two nails, and the prints of two nails were on the little feet.

'Who has dared to hurt you?' cried the Giant. 'Tell me, so that I may take my big sword and kill him.'

35 'No,' answered the child, 'these are the wounds of Love.'

'Who are you?' said the Giant, and he felt strangely afraid, and knelt before the little child.

The child smiled and said to the Giant, 'You let me play once in your garden. Today you shall come with me to my garden, which is Heaven.'

When the children ran in that afternoon, they found the Giant lying dead under the tree, all covered with white flowers.

4 The Model Millionaire

Hughie Erskine was a very good-looking young man. He was liked and admired by both men and women. He never said an unkind word about anyone. But he was not very clever, and never had any money. He was always changing his job and had tried everything. At one time he had worked on the Stock Exchange, which lasted for six months. He had been a tea merchant for a little longer than that, but soon got tired of selling tea. Then he tried selling sherry* instead, but again he failed. At last he gave up trying to work, and lived on two hundred pounds a year, given to him by an old aunt.

Now, he was in love with a girl called Laura Merton, who was the daughter of a retired Colonel. Laura loved him very much, and together they made a handsome couple. Of course neither of them had any money. The Colonel, although he liked Hughie, would not allow them to get married.

'Come to me, my boy, when you have got ten thousand pounds of your own, and we will see about it,' he used to say. Poor Hughie! He was very miserable.

The Painter

One morning, on his way to see Laura, Hughie called in to see a friend of his who lived quite near. His friend's name was Alan Trevor, and Trevor was a painter. He was a strange man, with a red beard. However, he was a very clever artist, and many people bought his paintings.

When Hughie came in, he found Trevor finishing the full-size picture of a beggar-man. The beggar himself was standing on a raised platform in a corner of the room. He was an old man, bent and wrinkled* with a pitiful look on his face. Over his shoulder he had a ragged brown coat, all torn and dirty. His thick boots were patched and well worn, and with one

**sherry,* a kind of wine.
**wrinkle,* small line on the skin of a person's face or hands.

hand he leant on a rough stick. In the other hand he held out a hat for money.

'What a wonderful model!' whispered Hughie, as he shook hands with his friend.

'A wonderful model?' shouted Trevor at the top of his voice. 'I should think so! You won't meet a beggar like him every day!'

'Poor old man!' said Hughie. 'How miserable he looks.'

'Of course,' replied Trevor. 'You don't want a beggar to look happy, do you?'

'How much does a model get for sitting?' asked Hughie.

'Ten pence an hour.'

'And how much do you get for your picture, Alan?'

'Oh, for this I get two thousand pounds!'

'Well, I think the model should get some part of that,' cried Hughie, laughing. 'He's working quite as hard as you.'

'Nonsense, nonsense. Why, look at all the trouble of putting on the paint, and standing up all day. It's not easy work I can tell you. Now do stop talking, I'm very busy. Smoke a cigarette and keep quiet.'

The model

After some time a servant came to tell Trevor that the frame-maker wanted to speak to him.

'Don't go away, Hughie,' he said, as he went out. 'I will be back in a moment.'

The old beggar-man sat down on a wooden seat that was behind him. He looked so lonely and sad, that Hughie could not help feeling sorry for him. He felt in his pockets to see what money he had. All he could find was a sovereign*.

'Poor man,' he thought, 'he needs it more than I do,' and he walked across the room and slipped the sovereign into the beggar's hand.

The old man jumped, and a faint smile crossed his lips.

'Thank you, sir,' he said, 'thank you.'

**sovereign*, a gold coin worth £1 sterling.

Then Trevor arrived and Hughie said good bye and left, feeling little silly at what h had done.

That night he wen to the Palette Club a about eleven o'clock and found Trevor havin a drink by himself.

'Well, Alan, did yo get the picture finishe all right?' he asked, a he lit a cigarette.

'Finished and framec my boy,' answered Tre vor, 'and you might lik to know that the ol model you saw like you very much. I had t tell him all about you who you are, where yo live, how much yo earn, what you are goin to do in the future –'

'My dear Alan,' crie Hughie, 'I shall prob ably find him at hom waiting for me. But c course you are onl joking. Poor old thing I wish I could do som thing for him. I thin it's dreadful that an one should be so mise able. I have got heaps c old clothes at home

do you think he would like any of them? Why, his rags were falling to bits.'

'But he looks so wonderful in them,' said Trevor. 'I wouldn't paint him in a good suit for anything. However, I'll tell him of your offer. And now, tell me, how is Laura? The old model was quite interested in her.'

'You didn't talk to him about her too,' cried Hughie.

'Certainly I did. He knows all about the Colonel, the lovely Laura and the ten thousand pounds.'

Surprise

'You told that old beggar all my private business?' cried Hughie, looking very red and angry.

'My dear boy,' said Trevor smiling, 'that old beggar, as you call him, is one of the richest men in Europe. He could buy all London tomorrow and never miss the money. He has a house in every capital city, eats off gold plates, and can prevent Russia going to war when he chooses.'

'What on earth do you mean?' cried Hughie.

'What I say.' said Trevor. 'The old man you saw today was Baron Hausberg. He is a great friend of mine, buys all my pictures and that sort of thing. He asked me a month ago to paint him as a beggar, and since he's paying, well I could not refuse. And I must say I think he made a splendid model.'

'Baron Hausberg!' cried Hughie. 'Good heavens! I gave him a sovereign!'

'Gave him a sovereign!' shouted Trevor, and he burst into a roar of laughter.

'I think you might have told me, Alan,' said Hughie crossly, 'and not let me make such a fool of myself.'

'Well, to begin with, Hughie,' said Trevor, 'I did not think that you went around giving away your money in that way. And really, when you came in I didn't know if Hausberg would like his name mentioned.'

'What a fool he must think me,' said Hughie.

'Not at all. He was very happy after you left. He kept laughing to himself and rubbing his old hands together. I couldn't understand why he was so interested in you at the time, but I see it all now. He'll invest* your sovereign for you Hughie, and pay you the interest every six months. He'll also have a good story to tell his friends after dinner!'

Hughie walked home feeling very unhappy, and leaving Trevor laughing loudly. 5

The next morning, as he was eating his breakfast, his servant brought in a card on which was written:

'Mr Gustave Naudin, messenger of Baron Hausberg.'

'I suppose he has come for an apology,' said Hughie to himself, and he told the servant to show the visitor in. 10

An old gentleman with gold spectacles and grey hair came into the room, and said with a French accent, 'Do I have the honour of speaking to Mr Erskine?'

Hughie bowed.

'I have come from Baron Hausberg,' he continued. 'The Baron – ' 15

'I ask, sir, that you will offer him my sincerest apologies,' cried Hughie.

'The Baron,' said the old gentleman with a smile, 'has asked me to bring you this letter,' and he held out a sealed envelope. 20

On the outside was written, 'A wedding present to Hugh Erskine and Laura Merton, from an old beggar,' and inside was a cheque for ten thousand pounds.

When they were married, Alan Trevor was the best man and the Baron made a speech at the wedding breakfast. 25

'Millionaire models,' remarked Alan, 'are rare enough, but model millionaires are rarer still!'

**invest*, to put money in a business to try to increase its value.

5 The Canterville Ghost*

When Mr Hiram B. Otis, the American Minister, bought Canterville Chase, everyone told him he was doing a very foolish thing. There was no doubt that the place was haunted*. Lord Canterville himself, a very honourable man, had felt it his
5 duty to mention the fact to Mr Otis, before he bought the house.

'We have not lived in the place ourselves,' said Lord Canterville, 'since my great-aunt went mad when two skeleton* hands were placed on her shoulders as she was dressing for
10 dinner. I must tell you, Mr Otis, that the ghost has been seen by several living members of my family, as well as by the Reverend Augustus Dampier, a well known man of the Church. After the unfortunate accident to my aunt, none of the younger servants would stay with us. And Lady Canter-
15 ville often got very little sleep at night, because of the strange noises that came from the corridor* and library.'

Mr Otis, however, laughed at these warnings, and bought the house. A few weeks later he and his wife, their son Washington, their daughter Virginia, and twin* boys, went
20 down to Canterville Chase.

When they arrived at the house an old woman was standing on the steps to meet them. This was Mrs Umney, the housekeeper, who had worked in the house for Lord and Lady Canterville.

25 'Welcome to Canterville Chase,' she said, and took them through the house to the library where tea was waiting for them.

**ghost*, a dead person who appears in the presence of someone living.
**haunted*, frequently visited by ghosts.
**skeleton*, the bony framework of the body, without flesh.
**corridor*, a long narrow passage in a house.
**twins*, two children born on the same day to the same mother.

The blood-stain

After they had taken off their coats and hats, they sat down while Mrs Umney poured the tea. Suddenly Mrs Otis caught sight of a dull red stain on the floor just by the fireplace.

'I'm afraid something has been spilt there, Mrs Umney,' she said. *5*

'Yes, madam,' replied the old housekeeper in a low voice, 'blood has been spilt on that spot.'

'How awful,' cried Mrs Otis. 'I don't care at all for blood-stains in a sitting room. It must be removed at once.' *10*

The old woman smiled, and answered in the same low mysterious voice.

'It is the blood of Lady Eleanore of Canterville, who was murdered on that very spot by her own husband, Sir Simon of Canterville, in 1575. Sir Simon disappeared nine years later *15* and his body has never been found. His guilty ghost still haunts the Chase. The blood-stain has been much admired by visitors to the house, and it cannot be removed.'

'That is all nonsense,' cried Washington Otis. 'Pinkerton's Stain Remover and Perfect Cleaner will clean it up very *20* quickly.' And before the housekeeper could interfere, he had fallen on his knees, and was rubbing the floor with a small black stick. In a few minutes the blood-stain had disappeared.

'I knew Pinkerton's would do it,' he cried, as he looked round at his admiring family. But as soon as he said these *25* words, a terrible flash of lightning lit up the room. A fearful crash of thunder made them all jump to their feet, and Mrs Umney fainted.

In a few minutes, however, she was able to sit up. There was no doubt that she was very unhappy, and she warned *30* Mr Otis that trouble could come to the house.

'I have seen things with my own eyes, sir,' she said, 'that would make your hair stand on end with fright. Many nights, I have not been able to sleep for the awful things that are done here.' *35*

Mr and Mrs Otis, however, told her that they were not

afraid of ghosts, and she at last went slowly out to her own room.

The Ghost

The storm blew fiercely all that night. The next morning, when they came down to breakfast, they found the terrible
5 stain of blood once again on the floor.

'I don't think it can be the fault of the Perfect Cleaner,' said Washington. 'I have tried it with everything. It must be the ghost.' He rubbed out the stain a second time, but the second morning it appeared again. The third morning it was
10 also there, though the library had been locked up all night by Mr Otis himself, and the key taken upstairs. The whole family were now quite interested.

That night they all went to bed at eleven o'clock, and by half past eleven all the lights were out. Some time later Mr
15 Otis was awakened by a curious noise in the corridor, outside his room. It sounded like the rattle* of metal, and seemed to be coming nearer every moment. He got up at once, struck a match and looked at the time. It was exactly one o'clock. The strange noise still continued, and with it he heard the
20 sound of footsteps. He put on his shoes, took a small bottle out of his case, and opened the door.

Right in front of him he saw, in the pale moonlight, a terrible old man. His eyes were as red as burning fire; long grey hair fell over the shoulders. His clothes, which were very old-
25 fashioned*, were dirty and ragged, and from his wrists and ankles hung heavy chains.

'My dear sir,' said Mr Otis, 'I really must insist on your putting some oil on those chains. I have brought you a small bottle of Tammany Rising Sun Oil. I shall leave it here for
30 you by the bedroom candles, and will be happy to bring you some more if you need it.' With these words the Minister laid the bottle down on a table and, closing his door, went back to bed.

**rattle*, a ringing sound.
**old-fashioned*, out of date.

Victories of the past

For a moment the Canterville ghost stood quite still. Then, throwing the bottle upon the polished floor, he ran down the corridor, making low groaning* noises, and glowing green in the darkness. Just as he reached the top of the great oak staircase, a door opened, two little children dressed in white appeared, and a pillow flew past his head. There was no time to be lost, so he disappeared through the wall, and the house became quite quiet.

On reaching a small secret room, he leaned against a moonbeam to get his breath back. Never, in all his three hundred years of haunting, had anyone been so rude to him. He thought of the Duchess whom he had frightened so badly as she stood before her mirror in her lace and diamonds. He thought of the four housemaids, who had screamed when he had smiled at them through the curtains of one of the spare bedrooms. Then there was the man whose candle he had blown out as he was on his way from the library, and who had been ill ever since. Old Madame Tremouillac, having woken early one morning, saw a skeleton sitting in an armchair by the fire reading her diary. She had been in bed for six months with an attack of brain fever. He remembered the terrible night when the wicked Lord Canterville was found choking* in his dressing-room, with a card half-way down his throat. He had confessed, just before he died, that he had cheated Charles James Fox out of £50,000 at cards by using that very card, and swore that the ghost had made him swallow it.

All his great victories came back to him again – the servant who had shot himself because he had seen a green hand tapping at the window. The beautiful Lady Stutfield, who had to wear a black velvet band round her neck to hide the marks of five fingers burnt upon her white skin. She had drowned herself in the fish-pond in the garden. He smiled as he remem-

**groan,* deep sound expressing pain or despair.
**choking,* being unable to breathe because of something in the windpipe.

bered the fuss he had caused when he played ninepins* with his own bones on the lawn-tennis ground.

And now, after all this, some awful Americans had come and had offered him the Rising Sun Oil, and had thrown pillows at his head! It was too awful. Besides, no ghost in history had ever been treated in this manner. He was determined to have his revenge*.

The changing stain

The next morning, when the Otis family met at breakfast, they discussed the ghost for some time. The American Minister was naturally a little annoyed to find that his present had not been accepted.

'I have no wish to do the ghost any harm,' he said. 'And I don't think it is at all polite to throw pillows at him, considering the length of time he has been in the house.' Here the twins burst into shouts of laughter. 'But,' continued Mr Otis, 'if he really refuses to use the Rising Sun Oil, we shall have to take his chains away from him. It would be quite impossible to sleep, with such a noise going on outside the bedrooms.'

However, for the rest of the week, there was peace. The only thing that happened was the continual re-appearance of the blood-stain on the library floor. This certainly was very strange, as the door was locked at night by Mr Otis, and the windows kept closely barred. The changing colour of the stain caused great excitement. Some mornings it was a dull red, then it would be brighter, then a rich purple. Once, when they came down for family prayers, they found it was bright green. These changes amused everyone very much, and they would all make guesses in the evening as to which colour it would be the following day. The only person who did not think the stain was funny was little Virginia. She, for some unexplained reason, was always upset at the sight of the blood-stain, and very nearly cried the morning it was green.

**ninepins,* game in which a ball is rolled along the ground at nine bottle-shaped pieces of wood.

**revenge,* do equal harm to somebody in return for a wrong done to oneself.

The second appearance of the ghost was on Sunday night. Soon after they had gone to bed they were suddenly frightened by a terrible crash in the hall. Rushing downstairs, they found that a large suit of old armour had come off its stand, and had fallen on the stone floor. And there, sitting in a high-backed chair, was the Canterville ghost, rubbing his knees, and with a look of great pain on his face. The twins had brought their pea-shooters with them, and they shot at him. Mr Otis pointed his gun at the ghost, and told him to hold up his hands!

The ghost jumped up with a wild scream of rage, and swept through them like a cloud. He put out Washington Otis's candle as he went, leaving them in total darkness. When he reached the top of the stairs, he opened his mouth and laughed his most horrible laugh, for which he was famous, until the walls shook. But he had hardly finished when a door opened, and Mrs Otis came out of her bedroom.

'I'm afraid you are not very well,' she said, 'and I have brought you a bottle of medicine. If you have stomach-ache, you will find this very good for it.'

The ghost stared at her angrily, and was just about to turn himself into a big black dog, when he heard footsteps. He disappeared, with a deep groan, just as the twins came up to him.

More hauntings

For some days after this, the ghost was very ill and hardly went out of his room at all, except to keep colouring the blood-stain. However, by taking great care of himself, he got better, and decided to make a third attempt to frighten the American Minister and his family.

He chose Friday, the 17th of August, for his appearance, and spent most of that day looking at his clothes. At last he put on a large, loose hat with a red feather, a white sheet which covered him from neck to toes, and he carried a rusty knife.

That evening it rained hard, and a fierce wind shook all the

doors and windows in the house. It was the sort of weather he loved. His plan of action was this. He would go quietly to Washington Otis's room, scream at him from the foot of the bed, and stab* himself three times in the throat to the sound of slow music. He especially disliked Washington, because he knew it was he who kept rubbing out the blood-stain. Having frightened that young man, his next stop was to be the bedroom of the American Minister and his wife. He would put a cold, wet hand on Mrs Otis's forehead, while he whispered horrible things into her trembling husband's ear.

He had not made up his mind about little Virginia. She had never been nasty to him in any way, and was pretty and gentle. Perhaps a few groans from the corner cupboard would be enough to waken her. As for the twins, he was quite determined to teach them a lesson. He would sit on their chests, to

**stab*, wound with a sharp pointed weapon.

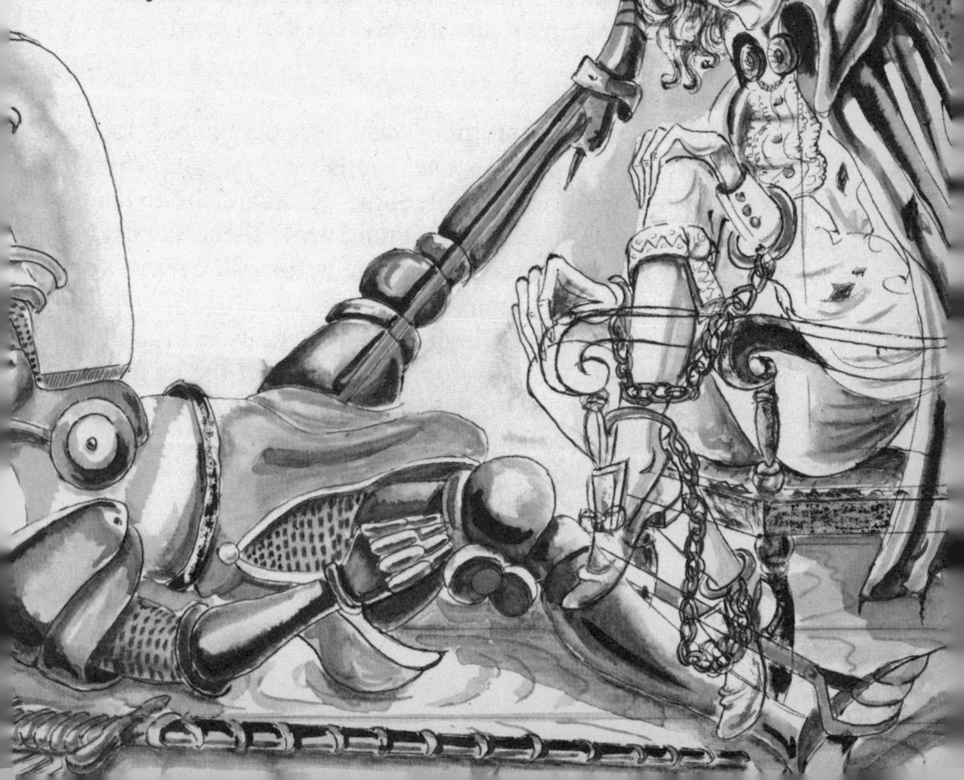

waken them, then stand between their beds in the form of a green, icy-cold corpse*. When they were stiff with fear, he would throw off his white sheet and crawl round on the floor showing his bones and one rolling eye-ball. This had been very successful in the past.

At half past ten he heard the family going to bed. For some time he was disturbed by wild screams of laughter from the twins, who were amusing themselves before they went to sleep. But at a quarter past eleven all was still, and at midnight he started out.

He stepped out of the wall, with an evil smile on his wicked face. The moon hid her face in a cloud as he crept along. Once he thought he heard something call, and stopped. But it was only the barking of a dog at the Red Farm. On and on he crept, like an evil shadow. Finally, he reached the corner of the corridor that led to Washington Otis's room. For a moment he paused there, the wind blowing his long grey hair about his head. Then the clock struck the quarter hour, and he felt the time had come to start. He laughed to himself, and turned the corner. As soon as he had done so, he fell back, with a scream of fright, and hid his face in his hands.

The second ghost

Right in front of him there was a horrible figure*. Its head was bald* and shining; its face round, and fat, and white. Its mouth was fixed in a horrible smile. Red light shone from its eyes and mouth, and it wore a long white sheet like his own. On its chest was a card with strange writing all over it, and in its hand it carried a shining sword.

As he had never seen a ghost before, he was naturally terribly frightened. After a second quick look at the awful thing, he ran back to his room, falling over his sheet on the way. He dropped his rusty knife into one of the Minister's boots, where it was found by the servants next morning.

**corpse*, dead body.
**figure*, shape.
**bald*, having no or not much hair.

Back in his own room, he threw himself down on a bed and hid his face under the clothes. After a time, however, he began to feel better and braver. He decided to go and speak to the other ghost as soon as it was daylight. So, just as the sun began to rise, he returned to the place where he had first seen the awful figure. He felt that, after all, two ghosts were better than one, and that, with the help of his new friend, he might be able to really frighten the twins.

When he reached the place, however, he saw something was wrong. Something awful had happened to the ghost, for the light had gone out of its eyes, and its sword had fallen from its hand. It was leaning up against the wall looking most uncomfortable. He rushed forward to catch it in his arms, when to his horror*, the head slipped off and rolled on the floor! He found himself holding a white bed-curtain, with a sweeping-brush, a kitchen knife and a hollow turnip* all lying at his feet! He could not understand this curious change in the other ghost, and took hold of the card which had been on its chest. And there, in the grey morning light he read these fearful words:

THE OLD GHOST

The Only True and Original Ghost.

Beware of Imitations.

All others are False.

Now he knew that he had been tricked. He raised his hand high and swore he would have his revenge. Then he went back to his room and stayed there until the evening.

A quieter ghost

The next day the ghost was very weak and tired. The excitement of the last four weeks was beginning to have its effect. He was nervous, and he was frightened by the tiniest

**horror*, feeling of extreme fear.
**turnip*, a large vegetable.

noise. For five days he stayed in his room, and at last made up his mind to give up colouring the blood-stain in the library. If the Otis family did not want it, they clearly did not deserve it. But it was his duty to appear in the corridor once a week, and he did not see how he could get out of it. So, for the next three Saturdays he walked the corridors as usual between midnight and three o'clock, taking every possible care against being seen or heard. He removed his boots, trod as lightly as possible on the old wooden floor, and wore a large black cloak. He was also careful to put the Rising Sun Oil on his chains. He was not very happy with this last method of protection. However, one night, while the family were having their dinner, he slipped into Mr Otis's room and carried off the bottle. He felt a little silly at first, but had to admit that it was better not to make so much noise.

Even so he was not left alone. Strings were continually being stretched across the corridor, and he tripped over them in the dark. And one time he fell very hard on a patch of butter, which the twins had made in the corridor leading to the top of the staircase. This last trick made him so angry, that he decided to visit the rude young boys the next night as 'The Headless Earl*'.

It took him three hours to make his preparations. At last everything was ready, and he was very pleased with his appearance. The big leather riding-boots that went with the dress were just a little too large for him. He could only find one of the two guns, but he was quite satisfied. At half past one he crept down the corridor.

When he reached the twins' bedroom, he found the door was open a little way. He wanted to give them a big fright, so he pushed it wide open. A large heavy jug of water fell right down on him, wetting him to the skin. It just missed his left shoulder by a couple of inches. At the same moment he heard screams of laughter coming from the beds. The shock he had suffered was so great, that he ran back to his room as fast as he could. The next day he had a bad cold,

**Earl*, an English nobleman.

and was thankful that he had left his head behind last night, or things might have been much worse.

He now gave up all hope of ever frightening this rude American family. He crept about the corridors in soft shoes, with a thick red scarf round his throat in case he caught a cold. He carried a small gun in case he should be attacked by the twins. The final shock he received happened on the 19th of September. He had gone downstairs to the entrance-hall, feeling sure that there he would be undisturbed. It was about a quarter past two in the morning, and, as far as he could tell, no one was awake. As he was walking towards the library, to see if there was any sign left of the blood-stain, two figures suddenly leaped out on him from a dark corner. They waved their arms wildly above their heads, and screamed out 'BOO!' in his ear.

He rushed for the staircase, but there he found Washington Otis waiting for him with a rubber water pipe. The only thing he could do was disappear, and he did – into the great iron stove, which luckily for him was not lit. He had to make his way home through the chimneys and reached his room very dirty and unhappy.

He must have gone

After this he was not seen again at night. The twins lay waiting for him several times, and put nut-shells in the corridors every night, but it was no use. It was quite clear that his feelings were so hurt that he would not appear.

The family now began to lead a more normal life. Mr Otis was able to get on with a book he had been trying to write for some years. Mrs Otis organized a wonderful party. The boys played American games. And Virginia rode out on her pony with the young Duke of Cheshire, who had come to spend the last week of his holidays at Canterville Chase. They all thought that the ghost had gone away. In fact, Mr Otis wrote a letter to Lord Canterville, who replied that he was very pleased at the news.

The Otises, however, were wrong. The ghost was still in the house.

Conversation with a ghost

A few days after this, Virginia and the young Duke went out riding. On the way, she tore her riding-dress badly in getting through a hedge. When she returned home, she went up the back stairs to avoid being seen.

As she was running past the Tapestry* Room, the door was open. She thought she saw someone inside. Perhaps it was her mother's maid, who sometimes brought her work there. So Virginia looked in, to ask her to mend her dress. To her great surprise, however, it was the Canterville Ghost himself! He was sitting at the window, looking out into the garden. His head was leaning on his hand, and he looked very sorry for himself. Virginia's first thought was to run away and lock herself in her room, but he looked so sad that she was filled with pity for him. She decided to try and comfort him. She trod so softly, that he did not realize she was there until she spoke to him.

'I am so sorry for you,' she said, 'but my brothers are going back to school tomorrow, and then, if you behave yourself, no one will annoy you.'

'It is stupid to ask me to behave myself,' he answered, looking round in great surprise at the pretty little girl who had dared to speak to him. 'I must rattle my chains, and groan through keyholes, and walk about at night, if that is what you mean. It is my only reason for being here.'

'You have been very wicked,' said Virginia. 'Mrs Umney told us, the first day we arrived here, that you had killed your wife.'

'Well, I admit it,' said the ghost, 'but it was a family matter, and nothing to do with anyone else.'

'It is very wrong to kill anyone,' said Virginia.

'My wife was very ugly,' said the ghost, 'and she never had my washing done properly. She could not cook, either. However, it does not matter now, for it is all over. And I don't think it was very nice of her brothers to starve* me to death, though I did kill her.'

**tapestry,* cloth with designs or pictures, made by weaving coloured threads into it, used for hanging on walls.

**starve,* to kill someone by refusing him food.

'Starve you to death? Oh, Mr Ghost, I mean Sir Simon, are you hungry? I have a sandwich in my case. Would you like it?'

'No, thank you, I never eat anything now. But it is very kind of you. You are much nicer than the rest of your nasty, 5 rude, dishonest family.'

'Stop!' cried Virginia, stamping her foot. 'It is you who are rude and nasty. As for dishonesty, you know you stole the paints out of my box to try to colour that blood-stain in the library. First you took all my reds, then the green and yellow. 10 I never told the others, though I was very annoyed. And it was most stupid, for who ever heard of green blood?'

'Well, really,' said the ghost, 'what could I do? It is very difficult to get real blood nowadays, and as your brother began it all with his Perfect Cleaner, I certainly saw no reason 15 why I should not have your paints.'

Virginia moved as if to leave the room.

'Please don't go, Miss Virginia,' cried the ghost. 'I am so lonely and so unhappy, and I don't know what to do. I want to go to sleep and I cannot.' 20

'Silly ghost,' said Virginia. 'All you have to do is go to bed and blow out the candle. It is sometimes difficult to keep awake, especially in church, but it is not at all difficult to sleep. Why, even babies know how to do that, and they are not very clever.' 25

'I have not slept for three hundred years,' he said sadly, and Virginia's eyes opened wide in wonder. 'For three hundred years I have not slept, and I am so tired.'

'Please help me!'

Virginia came towards him, and kneeling down at his side, looked up into his old lined face. 30

'Poor, poor ghost,' she whispered, 'have you no place where you can sleep?'

'Far away beyond the pine-woods,' he answered, in a low dreamy voice, 'there is a little garden. There the grass grows long and deep, and the birds sing all night long. The moon 35 looks down, and the yew-tree spreads out its great arms over the sleepers.'

Virginia's eyes filled with tears, and she hid her face in her hands.

5 'You mean the Garden of Death,' she whispered.

'Yes, Death. Death must be so beautiful. To lie in the soft brown earth, with the grass waving above one's head, and listen to the silence. To have no yesterday, and no tomorrow. To forget time, to forgive life, to be at peace. You can help 10 me. You can open the door of Death's house for me, for Love is always with you, and Love is stronger than Death.'

Virginia trembled, a cold shiver ran through her, and for a few moments there was silence. She felt as if she was in a terrible dream. Then the ghost spoke again.

15 'Have you ever read the old verse on the library window?' he asked.

'Oh, often,' cried the little girl, looking up. 'I know it quite well. It is painted in curious black letters, and is difficult to read. There are only six lines:

20 *When a golden girl can win*
Prayer from the lips of sin,
When the old almond tree bears,
And a little child gives away its tears,
Then shall all the house be still
25 *And peace come to Canterville.*

But I don't know what they mean.'

'They mean,' he said sadly, 'that you must weep for me and for my sins, because I have no tears. You must pray with me for my soul* because I have no faith. Then, if you have 30 always been sweet, and good, and gentle, the Angel of Death will have mercy on me. You will see fearful shapes in the darkness, and wicked voices will whisper in your ear. But they will not harm you, for Evil has no power over Good.'

Virginia did not answer, and the ghost waited anxiously as 35 he looked down at her bowed golden head.

Suddenly she stood up, very pale, and with a strange light in her eyes.

******soul,* **the part of a person which lives after the body dies.**

'I am not afraid,' she said firmly, 'and I will ask the Angel to have mercy on you.'

He got up with a faint cry of joy, took her hand and kissed it. His fingers were as cold as ice, and his lips burned like fire. He led her across the room. On the faded green tapestry there were little huntsmen. They blew their horns and waved to her to go back.

'Go back! little Virginia,' they cried, 'go back!' But the ghost held her hand more tightly, and she shut her eyes so that she could not see them. Nasty animals with lizard tails and huge round eyes looked at her from the wooden pictures round the chimney, and whispered, 'Watch out! little Virginia, watch out! We may never see you again.' But the ghost went on faster and Virginia did not listen. When they reached the end of the room he stopped and whispered some words she could not understand. She opened her eyes, and saw the wall slowly fading away, and a great black space in front of her. An icy cold wind swept round them, and she felt something pulling at her dress.

'Quick, quick,' cried the ghost, 'or it will be too late.' And in a moment the wall had closed behind them, and the Tapestry Room was empty.

Where is Virginia?

About five minutes later, the bell rang for tea. As Virginia did not come down, Mrs Otis sent one of the servants to tell her. After a little time he returned and said that he could not find Miss Virginia anywhere. Mrs Otis was not worried at first, for Virginia often went into the garden to pick flowers for the table, before the evening meal. But when six o'clock struck, and Virginia did not appear, she was really upset, and sent the boys out to look for her. She and Mr Otis searched every room in the house. At half past six the boys came back and said that they could find no sign of their sister anywhere.

Mr Otis then remembered that he had given some gypsies*

******gypsies*,** wandering people.**

permission to camp in the park. He set off on his horse to find them and question them. His eldest son and two of the farm servants went with him. The young Duke asked to be allowed to go too, but Mr Otis would not let him, as he was afraid there might be a fight. However, when he got to the camp, he found that the gypsies had gone, and in a hurry, too, for they had left a fire still burning and plates on the ground. He was worried that they might have stolen Virginia and taken her away with them. So, leaving Washington and the two men to search the district, he went home and sent telegrams to all the police inspectors round about, asking them to look out for a little girl who might have been kidnapped* by gypsies.

After this, he went to the station to see if anyone had seen his daughter, but no one had. The fish-pond in the grounds of Canterville Chase was searched, and so were the grounds themselves, but there was no sign of Virginia anywhere.

When he returned to the house, he found Mrs Otis lying down in the library and feeling very ill with worry. He insisted that she must have something to eat, and ordered supper for the whole family. It was not a happy meal, as hardly anyone spoke, and even the twins were quiet, for they were very fond of their sister. When they had finished Mr Otis ordered them all to bed, saying that nothing more could be done that night. Just as they were going out of the dining-room, a clock began to strike midnight. When the last stroke sounded they heard a crash and a sudden cry; a dreadful clap of thunder shook the house, strange music floated through the air, and a hidden door at the top of the stairs flew back with a loud noise. Out of the door, looking very pale and white, stepped Virginia, carrying a little box in her hand. In a moment they had all rushed up to her with cries of relief and delight.

The secret room

'Good heavens child, where have you been?' said Mr Otis,

**kidnap,* to carry away a person by force.

rather angrily, for he thought she had been playing some foolish trick on them. 'We've been looking for you all over the place, and your mother has been frightened to death. You must never do this again.'

'My darling, thank God you are found; you must never leave my side again,' said Mrs Otis, as she kissed the trembling child.

'Father,' said Virginia quietly, 'I have been with the ghost. He is dead, and you must all come and see him. He had been very wicked, but he was really sorry for all he had done. He gave me this box of beautiful jewels before he died.'

The whole family looked at her as if she was mad. Turning round, she led them through the opening in the wall down a narrow secret passage. Washington thoughtfully picked up a candle from the table before he followed them. Finally they came to a huge wooden door. When Virginia touched it, it swung back, and they found themselves in a little low room, with a vaulted* ceiling, and one tiny barred window. Stuck in the wall was a huge iron ring, and chained to it, was a thin skeleton. Its right arm was stretched out, so that it seemed to be trying to touch an old-fashioned jug and plate that were placed just out of its reach. The jug had once been filled with water, for it was covered inside with green mould*. There was nothing on the plate but a pile of dust. Virginia knelt down beside the skeleton, and, folding her hands together began to pray. The rest stood looking down at the terrible thing on the floor.

'Hallo!' called one of the twins, suddenly. He had been looking out of the window trying to find out whereabouts in the house this room was. 'Hallo! the old dry almond tree is in flower. I can see it quite plainly from here.'

'God has forgiven him,' said Virginia.

The funeral

Four days after these strange happenings, a funeral started

**vault*, a roof which rises to a point in the centre.
**mould*, a growth like fur which appears in damp places.

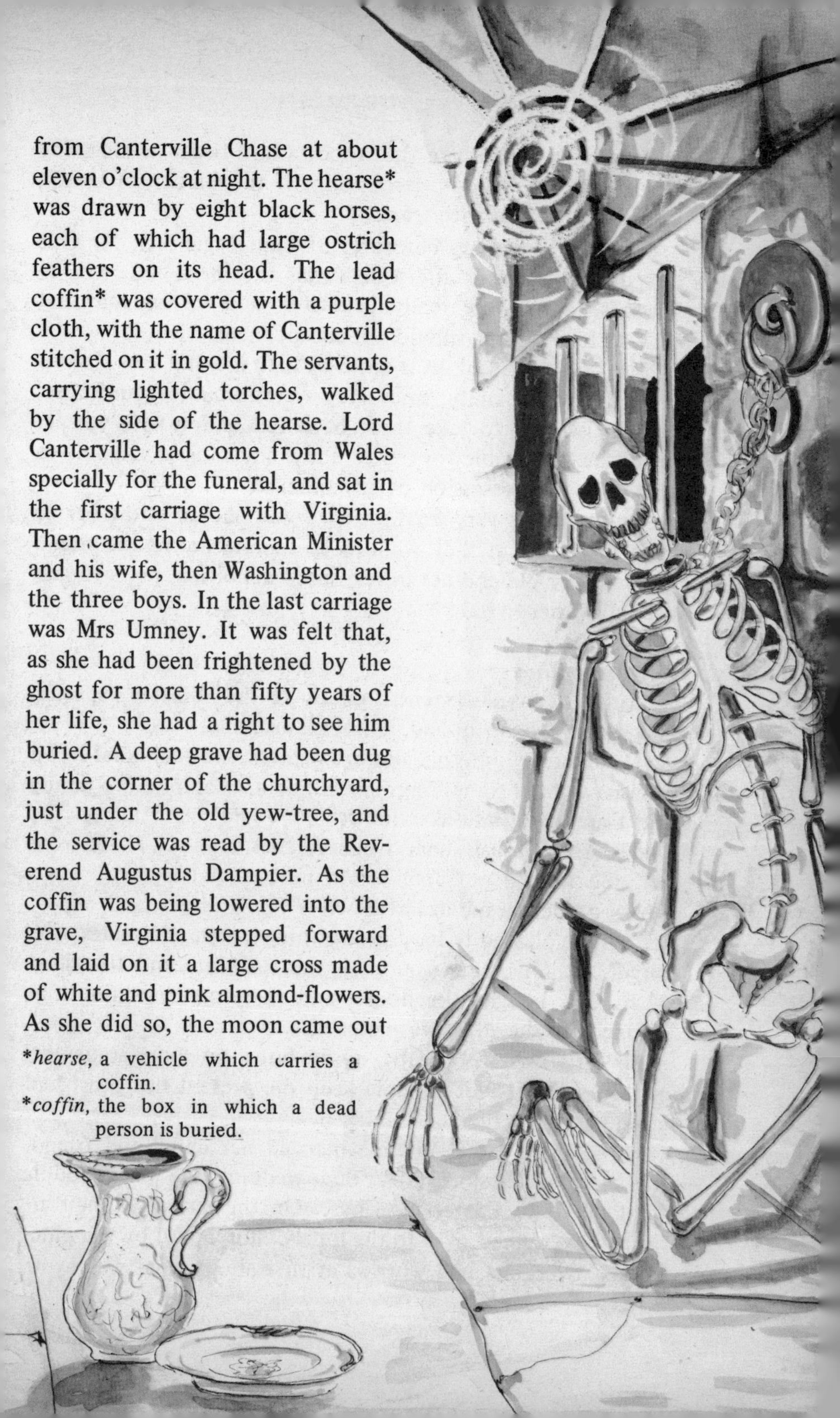

from Canterville Chase at about eleven o'clock at night. The hearse* was drawn by eight black horses, each of which had large ostrich feathers on its head. The lead coffin* was covered with a purple cloth, with the name of Canterville stitched on it in gold. The servants, carrying lighted torches, walked by the side of the hearse. Lord Canterville had come from Wales specially for the funeral, and sat in the first carriage with Virginia. Then came the American Minister and his wife, then Washington and the three boys. In the last carriage was Mrs Umney. It was felt that, as she had been frightened by the ghost for more than fifty years of her life, she had a right to see him buried. A deep grave had been dug in the corner of the churchyard, just under the old yew-tree, and the service was read by the Reverend Augustus Dampier. As the coffin was being lowered into the grave, Virginia stepped forward and laid on it a large cross made of white and pink almond-flowers. As she did so, the moon came out

**hearse*, a vehicle which carries a coffin.

**coffin*, the box in which a dead person is buried.

from behind a cloud. In the wood, a bird began to sing. She thought of the ghost's description of the Garden of Death, and her eyes filled with tears.

The next morning, before Lord Canterville left, Mr Otis talked to him about the jewels that the ghost had given to Virginia. They were really beautiful, and so valuable that Mr Otis felt Virginia should not accept them.

'My Lord,' he said, 'it is quite clear to me that these jewels belong to your family, since they were found in your house. I must ask you to take them back to London with you. It would be impossible for me to allow anything so valuable to remain in the possession of any member of my family. However, Virginia is very anxious that you should allow her to keep the box that they were in, to remind her of the ghost. As it is very old and not in very good condition, perhaps you may allow her to have it.'

A happy ending

Lord Canterville listened quietly to the Minister's speech, and when he had finished, he shook his hand.

'My dear sir,' he said, 'your daughter was very kind to Sir Simon, and did something very important for him. My family and I are very grateful to her for her courage and daring. The jewels are obviously hers. I believe that if I took them from her, the wicked old man would be out of his grave in two weeks bothering me again! When Virginia grows up I expect she will be pleased to have pretty things to wear. Besides, you forget, Mr Otis, that you took the furniture and the ghost when you bought the house, and therefore, anything that belonged to the ghost was yours also.'

Mr Otis was still greatly upset, but after some argument, at last agreed to let Virginia keep the present the ghost had given her.

Some years later, Virginia married her childhood friend, the Duke of Cheshire. After their wedding, the young couple went down to Canterville Chase. On the day after their arrival, they walked over to the lonely churchyard by the pinewoods. Everyone had worried at first about what was to be on Sir Simon's tombstone*. It had been decided to put on it the old gentleman's name, and the verse from the library window.

The Duchess had brought with her some lovely roses, which she placed upon the grave. They stood looking down at it for some minutes, then the Duke broke the silence. *5*

'Virginia,' he said, 'a wife should have no secrets from her husband.'

'Dear Cecil! I have no secrets from you.'

'Yes you have,' he answered, smiling, 'you have never told me what happened to you when you were locked up with the ghost.' *10*

'I have never told anyone, Cecil,' said Virginia slowly.

'I know that, but you should tell me.'

'Please don't ask me, Cecil, I cannot tell you. Poor Sir Simon! He made me see what Life is, and Death, and why Love is stronger than both.' *15*

The Duke kissed his wife lovingly.

'You can have your secret as long as I have your love,' he whispered. *20*

'You have always had that, Cecil.'

'And you will tell our children some day, won't you?'

Virginia blushed*.

**tombstone*, stone to mark a place where someone is buried.
**blush(ed)*, become red in the face from confusion or shame.

Questions

The Happy Prince

1. Why did the mothers want their children to be like the Happy Prince?
2. What had the little bird been doing since his friends left to go to Egypt?
3. When he got to the town, where did the bird go to sleep for the night?
4. When the Prince was alive he had been a rather selfish person. How can you tell?
5. Imagine you are the bird helping the Prince give his ruby to the mother and her child. Describe your journey over the city, and the scene in the poor house.
6. Why was the professor excited when he saw the bird?
7. How did the Prince's diamond help the young play-writer?
8. What happened to the other diamond?
9. What else did the Prince give to the poor?
10. Why was the statue pulled down?
11. What caused the Mayor and the Town Councillors to argue amongst themselves?
12. What did God send his Angel to find, and what did the Angel bring him?

The Star-child

1. How did the woodcutters find the Star-child?
2. Why did one of the men think his friend was foolish?
3. Why did the woodcutter refuse to go into his home at first?
4. What sort of person was the Star-child as he grew up?
5. Describe the Star-child's first meeting with his mother.

6. What did the Star-child's friends say to him when the old beggar-woman had gone?
7. What did the Star-child decide to do?
8. Who bought the Star-child, and what did he do to him?
9. How was the Star-child going to help the Magician?
10. Someone helped the Star-child to find the gold. Who helped him, and where did he find each piece?
11. He did not take the gold back to the Magician. Why not?
12. What happened to the Star-child because he had been kind to the beggar?
13. What did the people in the city want the Star-child to do for them? Why did he refuse?
14. What happened when he saw the beggar and the beggar-woman in the crowd?

The Selfish Giant

1. Why was the road not a good place for the children to play in?
2. Why was the Giant's garden always covered in snow?
3. The Hail and Frost liked the garden. Why do you think they were happy there?
4. The Giant heard a bird singing outside his window. What did this mean?
5. When the Giant went downstairs, where were the children?
6. How did he help the smallest child?
7. How did the little boy thank the giant for helping him?
8. When the Giant was old, the smallest child came back to the garden again. Why was the Giant angry when he saw him?
9. Who do you think the child was?

The Model Millionaire

1. Was Hughie Merton a good worker?
2. What did Hughie need before he could marry Laura?
3. Describe the beggar-man in your own words.
4. What did Hughie say to Trevor when he found that the artist was

paid two thousand pounds for his painting?
5. Did Trevor agree with him?
6. Why do you think the old man smiled when Hughie gave him the sovereign?
7. What did Trevor say the Baron would probably do with Hughie's sovereign?
8. Why did Hughie think that Mr Gustave Naudin had probably come for an apology?
9. What was the real reason for the Frenchman's visit?

The Canterville Ghost

Canterville Chase

1. How did Lord Canterville tell Mr Otis that Canterville Chase was haunted?
2. What was the first sign the family saw of any haunting?
3. How did Mrs Umney explain the presence of the stain?
4. What did Washington do to try to remove the blood-stain?

The Ghost

1. Describe what happened to Mr Otis after he went to bed on the third night.
2. What did the twins do to the ghost?
3. How had the ghost punished the wicked Lord Canterville for cheating?
4. 'He smiled as he remembered. . . . . ' What was it that made him smile?

The changing stain

1. What happened in the library to show that the ghost was still around?
2. How did Mrs Otis make the ghost angry?
3. What was the ghost planning to do on the night of 17th August?
4. What did the twins make that night?

A quieter ghost

1. How did the ghost try to make it easier for himself to move around without being disturbed?
2. What happened when he visited the twins' bedroom?

3. What took place on 19th September?
4. Why were the servants angry with the twins?

Conversation with a ghost

1. When she saw the ghost, Virginia wanted to run away. What changed her mind?
2. What had the ghost stolen from Virginia?
3. How did the ghost describe the Garden of Death?
4. How was Virginia going to help the ghost?

Where is Virginia?

1. What did Mr Otis imagine had happened to Virginia?
2. At what time did Virginia appear, and where?
3. When the family went to see the ghost, what did they find?
4. Why had the plate and jug been placed out of the reach of the person in the secret room?

The Funeral

1. Imagine that you are the Rev. Augustus Dampier. Describe the funeral procession and what happened in the churchyard.
2. Why did Mr Otis want Virginia to give the jewels to Lord Canterville?
3. Why did Mr Otis think that Lord Canterville might let Virginia keep the box in which the jewels were found?
4. What did Lord Canterville say would happen to him if he took back the jewels?

Oxford Progressive English Readers

Introductory Grade

Vocabulary restricted to 1400 headwords
Illustrated in full colour

The Call of the Wild and Other Stories	Jack London
Emma	Jane Austen
Jungle Book Stories	Rudyard Kipling
Life Without Katy and Seven Other Stories	O. Henry
Little Women	Louisa M. Alcott
The Lost Umbrella of Kim Chu	Eleanor Estes
Tales from the Arabian Nights	Retold by Rosemary Border
Treasure Island	R.L. Stevenson

Grade 1

Vocabulary restricted to 2100 headwords
Illustrated in full colour

The Adventures of Sherlock Holmes	Sir Arthur Conan Doyle
Alice's Adventures in Wonderland	Lewis Carroll
A Christmas Carol	Charles Dickens
The Dagger and Wings and Other Father Brown Stories	G.K. Chesterton
The Flying Heads and Other Strange Stories	Retold by C. Nancarrow
The Golden Touch and Other Stories	Retold by R. Border
Great Expectations	Charles Dickens
Gulliver's Travels	Jonathan Swift
Hijacked!	J.M. Marks
Jane Eyre	Charlotte Brontë
Lord Jim	Joseph Conrad
Oliver Twist	Charles Dickens
The Stone Junk	Retold by D.H. Howe
Stories of Shakespeare's Plays 1	Retold by N. Kates
Tales from Tolstoy	Retold by R.D. Binfield
The Talking Tree and Other Stories	David McRobbie
The Treasure of the Sierra Madre	B. Traven
True Grit	Charles Portis

Grade 2

Vocabulary restricted to 3100 headwords
Illustrated in colour

The Adventures of Tom Sawyer	Mark Twain
Alice's Adventures through the Looking Glass	Lewis Carroll
Around the World in Eighty Days	Jules Verne
Border Kidnap	J.M. Marks
David Copperfield	Charles Dickens
Five Tales	Oscar Wilde
Fog and Other Stories	Bill Lowe
Further Adventures of Sherlock Holmes	Sir Arthur Conan Doyle

Grade 2 (cont.)

The Hound of the Baskervilles	Sir Arthur Conan Doyle
The Missing Scientist	S.F. Stevens
The Red Badge of Courage	Stephen Crane
Robinson Crusoe	Daniel Defoe
Seven Chinese Stories	T.J. Sheridan
Stories of Shakespeare's Plays 2	Retold by Wyatt & Fullerton
A Tale of Two Cities	Charles Dickens
Tales of Crime and Detection	Retold by G.F. Wear
Two Boxes of Gold and Other Stories	Charles Dickens

Grade 3

Vocabulary restricted to 3700 headwords
Illustrated in colour

Battle of Wits at Crimson Cliff	Retold by Benjamin Chia
Dr Jekyll and Mr Hyde and Other Stories	R.L. Stevenson
From Russia, with Love	Ian Fleming
The Gifts and Other Stories	O. Henry & Others
The Good Earth	Pearl S. Buck
Journey to the Centre of the Earth	Jules Verne
Kidnapped	R.L. Stevenson
King Solomon's Mines	H. Rider Haggard
Lady Precious Stream	S.I. Hsiung
The Light of Day	Eric Ambler
Moonraker	Ian Fleming
The Moonstone	Wilkie Collins
A Night of Terror and Other Strange Tales	Guy De Maupassant
Seven Stories	H.G. Wells
Stories of Shakespeare's Plays 3	Retold by H.G. Wyatt
Tales of Mystery and Imagination	Edgar Allan Poe
20,000 Leagues Under the Sea	Jules Verne
The War of the Worlds	H.G. Wells
The Woman in White	Wilkie Collins
Wuthering Heights	Emily Brontë
You Only Live Twice	Ian Fleming

Grade 4

Vocabulary within a 5000 headwords range
Illustrated in black and white

The Diamond as Big as the Ritz and Other Stories	F. Scott Fitzgerald
Dragon Seed	Pearl S. Buck
Frankenstein	Mary Shelley
The Mayor of Casterbridge	Thomas Hardy
Pride and Prejudice	Jane Austen
The Stalled Ox and Other Stories	Saki
The Thimble and Other Stories	D.H. Lawrence